A SECOND CHANCE
Life Lessons Turned Into Living Dreams

by
Edison Jaquez

Copyright © 2015 Edison Jaquez
Cover Design: Tone Rodriguez
Edited by Stacey Debono
All rights reserved.

ISBN-13: 978-1516977604
ISBN-10: 1516977602

Dedication

I would like to thank God for making this book possible, my family for always being there for me, and all of the friends and mentors who have supported me along the way.

Introduction

Don't Let Your History Define Who You Are!

I made the decision to live by this because I refused to settle into stereotypes and misjudgments. Right now I can say I am in a happy place and I thank God everyday for my many blessings. Now, getting here was no easy task. I'd like you to venture through my journey and experience my highs and lows. We all have a story and it can be inspiring. I hope I can inspire you...

Chapter 1

On Wednesday, June 19, 2010, I had taken the day off from my job as a teacher's aide at one of Perth Amboy's middle schools. It was a decent gig and I enjoyed interacting with the students, but there were days when I needed a break. Or at least that's what I told myself, because I had been feeling particularly stressed recently. I was in my apartment with my two-year-old son, Armani, when my phone vibrated.

A message flashed on the screen from a familiar number, "Meet me in the parking lot at the middle school."

I hated getting those texts, asking for meet ups. I knew it was dangerous, but I had been selling drugs for almost a year now. I just needed a little more money, I told myself, then I'm going to quit. In the past couple of months I had acquired a few regulars. I was familiar and comfortable with the people I was dealing with. Business was smooth and I was almost on my way out. This client was new and made me feel edgy. It made this "easy" money not worth the stress.

This time, I had a bad feeling. "Yeah, well what are you gonna do about it?" I asked myself. This deal was going to earn a lot of money. I just wanted to get it over with, get the money, and get out of the game.

I left Armani in the apartment with a friend and walked over to the middle school. It was sunny, with a warm breeze. The kids had gotten out of school already and the grounds were quiet. I called the guy who'd sent the text. No answer.

"Where is this dude?" I muttered to myself. I wasn't feeling patient.

Minutes passed, feeling like hours, as the urge to "just get it over with" kept nagging at me. I wanted to get home, back to Armani. I saw a silver sedan pull into the lot. Finally. I headed towards the car. When I got up to the driver's window, I heard the sirens go off. Police cruisers pulled up all around me.

"Oh no. Please, no," I thought. This must be a nightmare. Slowly, I put my hands in the air.

Suddenly there was chaos all around me. It was surreal and I couldn't figure out how I got here. The police started yelling tons of questions at me but it all sounded faint and distant. All I could hear was the sound of my son's voice. How would I ever explain this to my son and his mother, Jennifer? How could I look them in the face? How did I let it come to this? They patted me down and found what they were looking for. They tried to intimidate me into giving up information and then they handcuffed me.

Sitting in the back of the cop car, my brain was heavy. I had been keeping my dealing a secret, no one else knew. But there was no more keeping it a secret now. I wonder what my parents would think? Would my parents be able to bail me out? I turned these questions over and over in my brain, numbly, while a realization of deep personal responsibility sank in. I made all the decisions that led to me sitting here, in the back of this car, right now. I might not like it, but I had to man up and accept it. This was ultimately my fault.

At the station, the detectives who had arrested me began threatening me, pushing me to give up my connects.

"You realize you'll get thirty years for this, right?" The detective had thin, reddish hair, and his face would turn the same color when he growled at me.

I sat there, shaking my head. "I want my lawyer," I responded.

A few hours of interrogation felt like an eternity. They threw me into a dirty holding cell. I then made my phone call, delivering the terrible news to Jennifer. Twelve sleepless, lonely hours later, some officers came and transferred me to Middlesex County Correctional Facility. County was dorm-style, with forty or fifty guys all in one large room. I was escorted to my bed with a change of beige pants, a white t-shirt and white tube socks. Anything else I needed, I would have to purchase. As I stood there, several guys from nearby bunks came over to introduce themselves. I exchanged greetings but I wasn't in the mood for conversation. Then I heard a voice say,

"Edison?"

I turned to see Jermaine, a younger brother who grew up with me in Stockton Street Projects. He was a couple grades behind me in school, but I had seen him often on the basketball courts.

"Hey man," I responded.

"Yo, I never expected to see you here man. You alright?" Jermaine asked.

"Yeah," was all I could manage.

Jermaine looked at me for a few seconds. "Alright man, well I'm over in the bunk by the left of the window. Let me know if you need anything."

"Thanks, man," I replied as I turned to find my assigned bunk.

Later that night, I would see other faces I knew from Stockton Street locked up in County. The next day I found myself sitting at a lunch table with five dudes from home.

"I still can't believe you're here." Jermaine said.

"I made bad decisions, man. I shouldn't have, but I did. This is what happens." I replied

"This brother was always doing the right thing," a dude named Tommy said to another, "Ain't you go to college?"

"Yeah, I did."

Tommy shook his head, as if he was truly at a loss for words. He didn't have to say it: "Well if this dude can't keep it straight, who can?" It reminded me—as if I needed reminding—just how much I'd let everyone down.

***

Seven days passed before my bail was reduced and my father was able to borrow the money to get me out. A good-natured family man who had worked hard his whole life, Papí's face was tense when he picked me up. We drove slowly back to my mother's apartment.

I slumped into a chair at the linoleum kitchen table. I was angry at myself, ashamed I had gotten myself into this situation. When my father sat down across from me quietly, I avoided meeting his eyes. My mother brought over some café con leche (coffee with milk) and sat down.

"Why'd you do it, *m'ijo*?"

"I wanted to put food on the table," I said, knowing this was a pitiful excuse. "Jennifer just started a new job, and I was working hard, but the money still wasn't enough."

"You couldn't pay the bills? Why didn't you ask for help?" Papí asked.

"I don't know. I didn't want to burden you and Mamí."

My father's eyes widened, incredulously. "You think I'd rather spend my money helping you out when you break the law? You know we would have done what we needed to for our grandson."

"I know, Papí. I made a bad decision, because of my pride."

Mamí was shaking her head. "Pride cometh before the fall," she quoted.

When they finally let me rest, I was so exhausted. When I got back to our apartment, Jennifer was quiet. The night I was arrested, she had come home to Armani in the arms of a friend of mine and some very bad news. She, too, had no idea what I was up to, and the hurt and anger she experienced was sudden and intense. Disappointment hung in the air. Still, she came over to give me a hug.

"I missed you," was all she said, with a heavy voice.

"I'm sorry. I am so angry I did this to you and Armani… but I'm going to make sure that you are both taken care of while I'm away. My friends will look out for you."

Jennifer took a deep breath. "Let's just make the best of the time you have left," she said.

I looked over at my son, who was playing with some toys in the corner. I went and sat on the bed by him.

"Look," he held up a red plastic fire engine.

"Yes, that's a Lightning McQueen fire truck," I said with a weak smile. I sat and watched him play with the truck, thinking about how I had hurt the people I was trying to protect. How was I so stupid to think that I was protecting them? I just wanted to be a good provider. Now what was I?

The school where I worked had terminated me, so the next day I went to a temporary agency looking for work. After a couple days they had a position on a warehouse loading dock for me. I saved as much of my paycheck as I could so Jennifer would have something to fall back on while I was gone. Still, there was no way I could save up enough to provide for everything they'd need. I could be gone for years.

It took two months for my case to go to trial. I was grateful for every day of freedom I had, but the mystery of my prison sentence hung heavily above me. Some days, I held my head high. "I am blessed," I'd tell myself, "I have a son, I have a family. I have to work hard to get back out there and build my life back up." Other days, I felt depressed. I'd worked so hard to earn my college degree and start a career, why did I just throw it away? It was going to be hard to get a good job with a record. My son would have a father in prison. How would I ever earn back the trust of my family?

For two months, I went back and forth, one day feeling like I'd overcome this and the next day like I'd lost something truly irreplaceable. Jennifer and I agreed to make the best of the time remaining, but she had made it clear that we would not be together anymore when I got released. "We'll always be family," she said, and she meant it.

My day in court was the worst day of my life. Jennifer, her sister Jessica, Armani, and my sister Kathy all sat behind me, dressed nicely in their church clothes, but with misery in their faces. No matter what happened, I was going to say goodbye to them today.

The judge was stern when he handed down my sentence.

"Mr. Jaquez, it disappoints me to see you come through my courtroom. You have a college degree, you have a family, you held down a job. And despite all those good choices, you threw it all away for some easy money. You say your good behavior deserves

my leniency, but I am truly concerned by your ability to ignore all the good in your life and make the decision to break the law. "
The truth of his words stung me deeply.

"I hereby sentence you to five years in New Jersey State Prison." I heard Jennifer gasp. I turned around to see my family crying.

Chapter 2

I was born in the Dominican Republic during the hottest month, when the warm waters of the Caribbean Ocean mean the beginning of hurricane season, August. Our yellow, cinder block house was located just outside the capital, Santo Domingo, on the south side of the island where tourists flock each year to see the historic Spanish architecture and glistening, white beaches. In the 1980s, however, tourists weren't yet a common site, and the island nation was suffering from decades of political corruption and oppression.

My father, Manuel, ran a little *bodega* (corner store), with a worn, blue concrete floor, on a cobblestone street in Kilometro 14. His little radio was always on, blasting *merengue*, *bachata* and *salsa* music for all who visited. Men from the neighborhood would stop by to hang out; chatting about baseball and telling jokes, for which my father always had a hearty laugh. He loved music, and on weekend nights he would put his saxophone in the back of his car and drive off to go play music with his bandmates at clubs in Santo Domingo.

On rainy days, my mother would put on his records for us while we played inside the three-bedroom house. On nice days, my little brother Emmanuel, whom we called "Eman", and I would leave the house as soon as we finished breakfast. We were always excited to play baseball and catch little green lizards in the perpetual warmth. Mamí knew all the women on the street, and she never thought twice about letting us out of her sight, confident there were always many watchful eyes in our neighborhood. The other boys and I would search for sticks to use as bats and the older boys would bunch up dried palm fronds and tie them tight into a ball so we could pretend we were Pedro Martinez as we played in the street.

When it was time to visit my *abuela*, my father's mother, Mamí would scrub us clean and dress us in our church clothes. My brother and I would sit in the back seat as Papí guided our car through the deep green countryside. On hot days, he'd pull over when he saw a *vendadero* (street vendor) and buy us little bags of fresh mango.

My *abuela*'s house was two stories, the wood painted white, with a screen door and a big porch. When we hopped out of the car, I could smell *tostones* (fried plantains) cooking inside. Abuela came out in her apron, walking over to shower her grandchildren with kisses and remark, "*Mira, mi negro lindo*, Edison!" When she bent down to kiss me, I'd scrunch up my face, preparing for an avalanche of kisses. Then, Mamí would let me and Eman run off to play in the tall grass and chase chickens while she and Papí would head inside to savor the smells of Abuela's kitchen as she prepared dinner.

The Dominican Republic is a third world country, riddled with poverty but rich in culture. Compared to other Dominicans, our family lived in luxury, but life in the Dominican Republic could be uncertain and corruption meant there were always public officials to be bribed for the privilege of operating a *bodega*. Although we had it relatively good, my father talked idealistically about the promise of a better life in the United States. Some of his friends and relatives had made the move, and sent back stories of good wages, American luxuries, and better educational opportunities for the children.

One day after dinner, my father remained seated at the wooden kitchen table, instead of going to his chair in the living room and putting on the radio, as was his ritual.

"I have some exciting news," he began addressing Eman and I. "We are going to move to *Nueva York*."

I was stunned. I looked at Eman, whose eyes were big with disbelief, but his mouth was wide in a toothy smile. How could he be excited? What about our friends? What about our school?

"No, Papí!" I blurted out. He gave me a stern look. I bit my lip.

"I know you don't want to leave, Edison, but that's because you don't know what *los Estados Unidos* will be like."

Mamí dried her hands on a kitchen towel as she walked over to put a reassuring hand on my back.

"You will make new friends, *m'ijo*. The American kids will like you."

I knew I'd get in trouble if I argued, but still I was worried. What about the friends I already had? Only seven years old, I didn't have any romantic notions about what the U.S. would be like. All I knew was my life in Kilometro 14; my friends, my house, my school. Why did we have to leave? I didn't even understand, at that point, that my new country would come with a new language to learn.

Soon, my aunts were helping us pack and my uncles were stopping by to pick up furniture and boxes of things we couldn't take with us. Little by little, our possessions dwindled, until there was nothing but a pile of suitcases and boxes, and my father was loading the car. I was quiet all the way to the airport, my brother and I dressed in tank tops and shorts. As our plane took off, I watched the green island I called home get smaller and smaller, until it was replaced by nothing but bright, blue ocean. When we arrived in New York, it was freezing cold and such a contrast to my warm and sunny hometown.

Our first week in New York City we stayed with my aunt in Brooklyn. The apartment was cramped with all of us there, and Mamí didn't want to let us play outside. Here, I heard sirens for the first time. After a few weeks, we moved again, this time to my maternal grandmother's apartment in Perth Amboy, New Jersey. It was here that Papí got a job in a warehouse and then we moved into our own apartment, our first one, a two-bedroom unit on the second floor of a nice building in Perth Amboy.

One night, Mamí burst into our bedroom, waking us all up, in her robe with her hair wrapped in a doobie, a way of straightening hair traditional in the Dominican Republic. Sleepy and confused, I knew something was wrong. The air smelled funny. She grabbed my new baby sister, Kathy, and Papí came in right behind her, scooping up my brother and grabbing my hand.

"Quickly, Edison, put your slippers on," he barked. I complied and he practically dragged me out into the hallway and down the stairs. When we reached the outside, I saw firetrucks in the street. I realized the men were coming towards our building. When we got to a safe distance and turned around, I saw flames leaping out of the windows of the upper floors. Kathy was crying and my mom looked like she would, too. My dad's hand gripped mine tightly. I wanted to run far, far away from the horrible sight. Instead, we stood there together and watched everything we had in America burn up.

This is how the Jaquez family came to reside on the eighth floor of the Stockton Housing Projects in Perth Amboy.

***

It's funny how clearly I remember the night of the fire. I remember feeling lost, not knowing what would happen next but knowing it wouldn't be good. In so many ways, this feeling was similar to what I felt when I got arrested.

Chapter 3

My first day in prison didn't feel real. I was sure this was all a nightmare and I kept praying I would wake up from it. Sleep was my strategy; I wished I could just sleep for the rest of my sentence.

I spent my first month in a holding cell in Craft for 23 hours a day. It was summer and the room was hot as hell. I had one roommate, Angel, a Puerto Rican guy who was a barber and drug dealer. At first I didn't feel much like talking, mostly because I was so miserably unhappy. But, boredom got the better of me, and Angel and I had a lot of hours to fill with trivial conversation.

"Where you from?" he asked.

"I grew up in Perth Amboy. Stockton Street Projects. You?"

"I'm from Newark man. Never been to Perth Amboy."

"It's small," I continued, "A lot of Latinos. There's a barber shop on every corner."

"Ha! Yeah. My neighborhood was like that," Angel said, "but the gangs and crime made a lot of them shut down."

A moment of silence passed.

"You got a family?" I asked.

"Yeah," he smiled, "I got a wife and a little girl, Ana. She's three. What about you?"

"I got a two-year-old son. His ma and I are taking a break right now, but I was still seeing him regularly before I got locked up," I said.

Angel nodded, "Cool. That's good you see your little boy a lot."

Angel had been to prison before, so he told me about what I could expect. After spending so much time in my tiny cell, I was almost looking forward to being transferred to a state prison.

Over a month passed before I was transferred. That morning, we woke up early and the guards cuffed us. We walked slowly, single file, to a waiting bus.

As we drove, I stared longingly out the window, watching the sunrise on the free world. I thought about Jennifer and Armani, wondered how they were doing. When I saw Annandale State Prison on the horizon, my heart sank into my stomach. Layers of tall, razor-wire fences, gun turrets, and sinister looking gates gave me chills. The ominous place grew bigger and bigger until we were entering a series of gates. Inside, the bus stopped and we were directed to unload, single file, and march into a low building.

Inside, prison staff gave us two changes of clothes, two towels, washcloths, a toothbrush and toothpaste. Next, they shuffled us into a large room with bright florescent lighting, where we spent the next three to four hours in orientation about prison life.

As the guard explained the rules and regulations, I couldn't believe how many young men sat there with such an easy going, laid back attitude. They listened and didn't even seem phased by all the restrictions. At one point the guard asked us how many of us had been there before. I was shocked to see how many repeat offenders were among us. I knew this was one place to which I would never be returning.

When the orientation was over, we were assigned bed numbers and released to go find our beds. Annandale was dormitory style, like County had been, with about 30 guys to a room. I walked into a large room with cinderblock walls, painted light grey. Metal bunk beds with thin mattresses were spaced out evenly, and low walls divided the space around the bunks into small cubicles. Each bunk had a number printed on it. I found mine, a top bunk. A young man was relaxing on the bottom bunk, lying on top of the blanket. He looked me over before he spoke.

"Welcome to Annandale," he opened.

"I would say thanks, but it ain't anything to be thankful for," I joked back.

"What's your name?"

"Edison. Yours?"

"Rashawn. I'm from Jersey City."

I nodded, "I'm from Perth Amboy, man." I looked around, still holding my change of clothes, towels and toothbrush. "Where can I put my stuff?"

Rashawn raised an arm, pointing at a cluster of lockers against the low, dividing wall. "You got the one second from left E."

A few minutes later, a new group of inmates approached us. The prisoners had their own orientation for new arrivals. Three of the older, well-respected inmates gave us the tour and explained their version of how things work around here. They told us what cliques to stay away from, which inmates are trouble makers and which guards to play nice with.

At the end of the day, I was looking forward to calling Jennifer. Her voice made me homesick.

"Hello Edison, how are you doing?"

"I'm okay, Jennifer. I'm just getting adjusted to this place..." I didn't know what else to say. How do you explain all of these terrible feelings and new experiences happening all at once? I gasped, "How is Armani?"

"He's good. He's playing with his toys right now." She called him over to the phone. "It's Dada, baby. Say hi."

I softened my voice, "Hey little man, how are you?"

Armani was shy on the other end. I told him, "I miss you so much. I hope I can see you soon."

I heard him say something softly to Jennifer. She returned to the phone. "He says he misses you, Edison."

Even though Armani couldn't speak yet, he was so used to me being around and certainly felt my absence. We used to go to sleep together, and wake up together. My heart was heavy. I told Jennifer about the visitation rules and we made plans for her and Armani to come visit that weekend. When I laid down that night, I wanted to slip quickly into the oblivion of sleep, but sleep didn't come. My heart was heavy with loneliness. Memories played out in my mind as I lay there, wide awake and exhausted.

***

March 5, 2008. I was working and going to college. I'd spend all day at work, rush home to change my clothes after I got off, and run out the door to catch the bus to school for evening classes. I was determined to make it through college, to prove every person wrong who said I wouldn't amount to anything. But it was an exhausting schedule, and I wasn't making enough for us to get by. On top of it, Jennifer and I were expecting a baby.

I got home that night, ready to fall into bed but with homework assignments to complete. It was around midnight, and I was up late solving math problems by the lamplight when I heard Jennifer cry out in the bedroom.

Her voice was strained. I jumped up and rushed into the room. She sat upright in the bed, her eyes wide in shock.

"Edison… I'm getting bad contractions!"

I rushed around the house, grabbing shoes, coats, everything we needed to rush to the hospital. I helped her out to the car, moving slowly, and then rushed back inside for some forgotten items. While in the car, contractions started coming regularly. I drove faster, my girl looking pained.

At the hospital, I stood by the bed. Her labor was long but she stayed strong and delivered our eight pound baby boy at 12:24 pm.

"Would you like to cut the cord, Daddy?"

The doctor held scissors up for me. I was so nervous I almost cut the umbilical cord incorrectly. The nurse cleaned and dressed our baby boy, and when she placed his tiny body in my arms, tears of joy stung my eyes. This fragile little person, he was part of me and I was part of him. Everything he needed, he would look to me for. I felt a change as I gazed at him. The world suddenly seemed more real—more important, more dangerous, more beautiful, but above all, I immediately felt more responsible. It was my job now to make everything right for him.

Jennifer's sister, Jessica, was taking pictures, capturing every moment. The first person I called was my boy, E.K., to spread the news. When I went home that day, leaving Jennifer and the baby in the hospital for the night, I started preparing every little detail so we could bring Armani Lexzander Jaquez home.

***

In prison, there is a weird loneliness. You're always surrounded by people, always talking, joking, and singing.

Sometimes, that's enough distraction to slip away into the moment, to laugh, to join in the conversation or to just get lost. Yet, in many ways, you are completely alone. There are no family or friends around to help you get through things. When you really start thinking about home, that is when you are the loneliest.

When the weekend came, I was so excited for Jennifer and Armani to visit me at Annandale. Looking forward to it kept me going all week, and even my neighbors noticed I was cheerful that morning.

The visiting room was white, with small tables and plastic chairs evenly spaced and bathed in florescent lighting. To go in and out, you had to be searched. The visiting room was no break from the rules either. You could hug your guest twice; once in the beginning and once before they left. There was no touching during the visit. All the while, correction officers stood around the room, watching everyone.

Jennifer held Armani in her arms as she approached me, and we all embraced before sitting down. Seeing my little boy's face made me so happy that I forgot for a moment where I was.

"Thank you for coming. It is so good to see you." I began as we sat down at a small plastic table.

"Of course. How are you doing?" she asked.

"I'm holding up. It still feels like a bad dream, but every time I wake up, I'm still here," I chuckled.

Armani was wriggling around in Jennifer's arms. He wanted to get down and walk around, but that wasn't allowed.

"I put some money in your commissary account. Did you get it?"

"Yes, thank you for that. I bought some ramen noodles yesterday, it tasted so good! The food here is awful."

Armani was starting to get frustrated. He began to cry. Jennifer tried to quiet him, but he was just too young to understand the situation. All he knew was he wanted to walk around and Mommy wasn't letting him.

"What about you, how are you doing?" I asked.

"I'm alright. It's tough, Edison. I have my mom taking care of Armani when I'm at work, so that helps."

"I know, I'm so sorry I put you through this..."

Jennifer smiled but her eyes were sad. She shrugged. Armani was still shifting around, trying to break out of his mother's grasp.

"Can I hold him?" I asked, looking at the correction officer. He nodded in approval, so Jennifer passed Armani over.

"Hey little man," I said softly, holding him up.

He was busy looking all around the room, and soon he was struggling to get down and walk around again. After twenty minutes, it was clear that the visiting room of a state prison is no place for a toddler. As much as I needed to see him, I told Jennifer not to bring him back. My responsibility as a father was always to do what's best for him, even though it would hurt me.

Chapter 4

When you're dealing with the guilt of having done something reprehensible, and you know that you've hurt your family, it's easy to slip into self-loathing. I was angry at myself for landing in prison and I wasn't able to forgive myself.

One day I called Jennifer. The phone calls are limited to only 15 minutes, so you have to be ready to say what you want to say. But I was depressed, and I wanted to call her because I was desperate to hear some gentle words.

I told her, "That's it, my life is over. My bachelor's degree means nothing. All that sacrifice, all the late nights and early mornings, all that I worked so hard to achieve… now I took it away from myself."

She said, "Edison, I know this is hard and you can't see it now, but God can turn this around."

I wanted to believe her, but I couldn't see it yet. It didn't help that I had nothing but time, more hours in a day than I could ever fill, and every day stretched out before me, dragging by painfully slow. When you're in that dark place of self-hatred, many hours a day you spend criticizing yourself, feeling terrible, feeling useless. I tried to sleep as much as I could; I wished I could've slept 24 hours a day until my sentence was over.

Although men of all ages wind up in prison, an alarming majority of the inmates were young, just 18 or 19. These young men had already spent time in juvenile facilities and were finding themselves stuck in a revolving door between prison and their own impoverished neighborhoods. At 27 years old, I was almost a decade older than these men. Naturally, a couple young men in the bunks near mine tried coming to me for advice. But I turned them away; I was too overwhelmed with my own problems to be able to help them with theirs. It was selfish but I just lacked any positive words to say.

A young brother, Robert, had gotten assigned to serve lunch in the cafeteria. Robert started off playing favorites; he'd give more food to his friends and others would get skimped. This was understandably making the inmates who got shorted upset. Robert was heading for trouble. One day, I was hanging out with him in the yard, and I decided to bring it up.

"Robert, how long are you in for?"

"Four years." Robert was just 18 years old, so this meant he'd spend his formative years as a young man in prison.

"That's a long time. You know your stay here is all about the people, right? You don't want to start making enemies now."

"What are you talking about?" he replied.

"You been giving out the food unequally," I explained. "The folks who aren't getting as much are getting mad at you."

"Man, I'm just looking out for my homies, know what I'm saying? They watch my back and so I take care of them."

"I know you want to look out for your boys, but you've been given a position of authority. You're abusing it by not giving the food out fairly. You are going to cause more trouble for yourself in the long run."

Robert thought about it for a minute, and said he understood what I was saying and changed his ways. A couple of weeks later, he came back to me to say thanks. Robert had noticed he was having a lot less problems with the other inmates, and he was happy things were going smoothly.

A few weeks later, I received my own job assignment. I was to become a teaching assistant for the prison's education program. The men who enrolled had almost zero chance at legal employment without a diploma or certificate. I sensed they wanted help getting an education and planning a path for success, but they doubted their own abilities. Others in their lives had given up on them, but they weren't ready to give up on themselves.

As we went through the first weeks of the course, I found myself giving words of encouragement to the students, along with coursework help. Slowly, it dawned on me that the advice I was giving to others was helping me as well. My thoughts about my own life began to shift toward the positive. Telling others to believe in themselves meant I had to believe in myself as well. To do otherwise would be hypocritical.

Practicing what you preach is called integrity. To understand what is the right course of action but not act on it, is self-destructive. When you live with integrity, it means you not only understand something is the right course of action, but you accept and live by that truth. When you begin to practice living with honesty and sincerity, you build more integrity. So, I decided to buy a small, blue notebook at the commissary. I began spending my time in my bunk, writing out my thoughts.

Sometimes I wrote what I wanted to do, my vision for the future. "I will take my son to the park," I wrote on a list of things I wanted to do when I returned to my life on the outside. "I will spend more time with Mamí and my family."

The notebook helped me pass the days. Over time, I began to get more specific with what I wrote down. My small visions were now becoming specific goals. "I will go to the library and take the time to update my resume", and "I will spend all day applying for jobs."

I also wrote to get feelings off my chest. I wrote about my anger at myself. Seeing those harsh words on paper made me realize I'd have to find a way to forgive myself in order to move forward.

***

When I was young, starting in 5th grade, our school partnered with an after-school program run by Catholic Charities that set up trips for us to go hiking and camping during the summer. My friends and I loved those trips. Participation was contingent on good behavior, so I would encourage my friends to stay out of trouble so we could all go. They would say the same thing to me, although my desire to go was so strong that I didn't need much reminding.

The program coordinator was a young Boricua woman named Sandy. She had grown up in Perth Amboy, and she came back after college with the intention to give back to her community. Sandy was patient and nurturing when she needed to be, but she also had a sharp tongue for the kids who tested her boundaries. "If you came to this program looking for trouble, you're going to get kicked out, no questions," she'd often remind us. Many who tried the program coordinator job before hadn't lasted long, but Sandy knew how to handle the kids growing up in the Stockton Street Projects. Still, she had a natural warmth and positivity that would return right after she scolded someone, like the sun coming back out from behind a cloud.

Sandy always talked about choices. She reminded us often: If you come to this program and you're looking for trouble, you're going to get kicked out. If you come here and you want to learn and go on these trips, you will get to go. The choice is yours. If you behave and don't disrespect, you get to go on trips. Inevitably, someone would get in trouble and lose the privilege of going on the next trip. When I was in 7th grade, my buddy Joey got detention just a couple weeks before we were supposed to go camping in Pennsylvania.

"I'm sorry to hear you won't be able to go," she said to Joey when she found out. There were about ten of us assembled in her office. Joey's eyes were cast down at the floor.

She asked him, "Did you learn something today?" Joey nodded. "What did you learn?" she pressed him.

"I have to do my homework and stay out of detention so I can go on the next trip," he muttered softly.

"You all heard that? Because Joey didn't do his homework, he won't be going on our camping trip. Does anyone else want to join him?" The rest of us shook our heads vigorously, not saying a word.

The hiking trips took us far outside of the world we were used to, into the green wilderness with everything we needed in a backpack. Our parents couldn't take us to places like this. Once we got out into nature, our toughness would melt away. Cooperation was more important, and we were afraid of running into a bear. We got to make our own campfire, roast marshmallows, and be kids.

***

Once I reached high school, getting in trouble was becoming a regular occurrence. My friends and I would get into fights, stay out late, and we fell behind on our school work. My family and others would tell me I wasn't going to make it far the way I was acting. They said I wouldn't graduate high school, that I wouldn't make anything of my life. Their harsh words motivated me to prove them wrong, and not only did I get my high school diploma, which I had to go to summer school for, but also attended college afterwards.

Sandy had been promoted to counselor in the high school, and she was a person I went to when I needed to talk. She helped teens with their homework and with filling out college applications. At the end of my senior year, my grades weren't good and I needed to go to summer school to graduate. My teachers told me, "you're not college material." My family had always taught me that school was important, but college was a high goal that they didn't speak of much. Sandy, in contrast, would say "Edison, you can be anything you want. If college is what you want, you should go for it." She knew my terrible grades were due to my behavior, not my ability.

Looking back, I can see there is a difference between being externally motivated to do something versus being internally motivated. I was externally motivated by my naysayers in high school. I didn't necessarily care about getting my diploma for myself and my future. I desired to prove the people wrong who said I couldn't. When I was younger, I was internally motivated to go on those hiking and camping trips. I wanted to experience those for myself, and I was willing to do what it took to make those trips a reality.

Sitting in prison, I realized I had to return to that internal source of motivation to get back on my feet and get my life back together. I had to want things because I wanted them for myself. I had to set myself on a path to achieve those things I wanted.

Chapter 5

Prison is full of people who've gotten used to being defined by their worst. It's an environment that's very negative because people have accepted that. Most don't have a positive example in their life otherwise, as their role models are incarcerated too.

Some of them are leaders who speak with confidence, stand up straighter, and take control of situations. Many more are followers, who wait for others to act and do what they are told. People are lost when they first arrive, and they look for ways to adapt. The trouble is adapting too well. Many of the people in prison are actually resilient people, having been through a lot, but they lack resources. Reflecting on this made me realize I had been a follower in many ways. I wanted to be accepted by my peer group, and when I was younger, by the older boys. We looked up to drug dealers because they gave us money for food, and because they were always watching out for the neighborhood. We didn't see the late night drug sales, not until we grew up and started selling. I was a follower because I knew right from wrong, and I made a conscience decision to choose wrong. I was acting out so I could live up to a negative label and be "cool". I was hanging out late, missing curfew, getting in fights.

One time, me and my friends Richie, Robbie, Joey, Danny and Terrance went to the movies and we didn't go home afterwards. We just hung around, talking shit, and walking in the area of the theater. I knew I was violating the curfew set by my parents, but I wanted to stay out. I told myself, "I can do what I want." A cop cruiser pulled up and flashed its lights. We stopped. The officer stepped out and walked over to us.

"What are you fellas doing out here?" he asked.

We were all silent, waiting for the other to speak. "We're just hanging out, Officer. We just got out of a movie."

"The movies were over a while ago. Where do you boys live?" he responded.

That night, we each got escorted home in a paddy wagon. He said he did it to get us off the street and to teach us a lesson. He walked each of us up to the door and told our parents he'd found us loitering late at night. My parents were livid.

"You think that's okay, Edison? Just hanging out late, you're looking for trouble!" Papí said. He was already going for his belt.

"Coming home in the back of a cop car," Mamí got started, "I thought I'd have a heart attack!"

I got a whipping that night. After that I was more careful not to get caught hanging out on the street, but I kept staying out late.

***

Teaching the GED class in prison made me feel like I was back to my outside life. Most of my students were young, almost 10 years younger than me. They couldn't do math or read well, but they had the drive to learn it, and I was going to help them reach their goal. The problem was that they had never been taught how to do these things, not that they were stupid. I knew that and I told them all they had to do was learn.

When I first came to America, I had a hard time making friends because I only spoke Spanish. My first friends were other Dominicans and I felt silly and embarrassed when I spoke English. Over time, I learned more and more English and I made English-speaking friends. All I had to do was learn. So I told my students to be patient with themselves because it takes time to learn how to do something new.

After class one day, a slender, tattooed young man named Jiminez came up to the front of the room to talk to me.

"I used to feel silly when I was learning English, too," he confessed to me with a smile.

"How old were you when you came to the States?" I asked.

He thought for a second. "Probably about 8 or 9."

"I was 7 myself. It takes longer to learn when you're older," I said, "My baby sister was born here and learned English from making friends outside of our house."

"Yeah, I have a little brother like that, too," Jiminez replied, "Anyways, that comparison makes sense to me. Math is so hard for me but I have to learn it to pass this GED test."

"I bet your family will be very proud of you when you get that degree," I said.

Jiminez smiled faintly. "Yeah." We started walking out of the room and down the hallway.

"What do you want your life to be like when you get out?" I asked him.

"I don't know, man. I just… I don't want to come back here. But I don't know if I can even find a job."

"Listen," I said, "You can find a job. But just like this GED class, you have to be patient and not give up. Once you get your GED, it will be easier to find work but you still have to be persistent."

Jiminez shrugged. His eyes were gazing down towards the floor.

"Focus on one thing at a time," I advised him, "Learn the math and get your GED. Once you do that, you can focus on thinking about different jobs you can do. Myself, I got a little notebook and I write down my ideas for what I will do when I get out. It helps me stay focused on turning this negative into a positive."

"Oh, word?" Jiminez looked up at me, "Maybe I'll try that."

***

Learning English was not the hardest thing for me to get used to once my family moved to the United States. It was the terrible conditions at the Stockton Street projects after the fire--the smell of urine in the elevator, the drug addicts in the hallway, the roaches everywhere. Although mi familia never had a lot, we had never lived around things like that. I started acting out soon after we moved in, getting in trouble, not doing my homework, and fighting other boys at school.

My parents, especially my Mamí, were determined to make the best of the situation. While the world outside might have been depressing, inside our apartment was like taking a trip to the Dominican Republic with bright and colorful decorations, joyful Spanish music and the mouth-watering aroma of foods like *sancocho*, *mofongo*, and *moro de habichuelas*. Although we didn't have a lot, my parents would always share whatever they had to give, joyfully. It wasn't long before our apartment was a favorite among my friends, many of whom didn't have anyone to cook fresh meals for them. Papí would tell my friends stories about his home country and remark that America was too materialistic.

"You kids have enough to get by on," he'd say, "Why do you think you have it so bad?"

I made a lot of friends through sports, which I played all year round. Baseball, football, and basketball kept me busy and that's how I met a lot of kids from different backgrounds. I met many that had more difficult struggles in their lives, no parents or no food in the house. Through my parents, I learned how to be caring and to listen to other people's stories.

Being incarcerated, I had to put on a mask. I couldn't be the nice person, treating people well. I had to act tough and be aggressive, like I didn't care what I did. The GED class was the only place I could let my guard down, and listen to people. And it was through my students that I was helping myself sort out the reasons I ended up here and how I too could turn things around, just like I was assuring my students they could.

Visits with my family were the only other time I could let my guard down and be myself. I looked forward all week to those visits, and all I wanted to hear about was what was going on outside these walls I was stuck inside. When you have visitors coming, everyone waits in a big room outside the visitor area, and waits for their name to be called. Jennifer had told me she was coming and was bringing Armani with her. I waited patiently. Thirty minutes passed, then forty-five. At first I was calm, thinking she had gotten held up leaving, or maybe there was more traffic than usual. As the time stretched out longer and longer with no word, my calm dissolved into anxiety. What if something had happened to them? What if they had an accident? The visiting hours passed by without my name being called, and then I was worried. When my buddy Jason asked me what was up, I snapped at him. Then I went back to my bunk to try to sleep off my bad mood.

The next day, I wrote a letter to the prison counselor. He responded with an explanation: Jennifer had been turned away because the guard on duty thought her jeans were "too tight". A few days later, I received a letter from Jennifer. She had to turn around and drive an hour and a half hours back to Perth Amboy; there is no use arguing with a correctional officer as you'll just get banned from visiting, period.

Chapter 6

After a few months in Annandale, I was transferred to Bordentown. As soon as I got there, I ran into my friend Duke and a few others from back home, and I knew I was going to be alright. While I was there, I made new friends with others who were good guys. Sonny and Harlem were two guys that made sure I was good and we have remained like brothers ever since.

In prison, the authority of the guards is absolute and the prisoners have none. You shower when they say shower, eat when they say eat, walk where they say to walk. The funny thing is, everyone who ends up in prison is there because they rejected authority, or thought it didn't apply to them. Myself, I thought I was slick and too smart to get caught. I thought, if I just sold for a little while, I could earn some money and quit before I got caught. Now, I had to admit I had been arrogant and that arrogance had cost me dearly. The law was not the only authority I had disrespected. My decisions had gone against the wisdom and love of my family and my elders.

When I was about eleven, I started playing basketball in a league coached by Bobby Nicholson. Bobby ran the after-school program through the housing authority and I earned a spot on the team. Bobby was a friendly, fatherly man, tall and big with a warm smile. He was active in his church and in the community. Several of my good friends were on the team, too, including Richie, Terrance, and Robbie. We'd travel all over the city and nearby areas to play games, which was much further than we usually got outside our neighborhood. We were accustomed to fighting, because, in our neighborhood, you had to fight to show you're not weak or else you got teased. Some kids fought because they hadn't had anything to eat but school lunch. Sometimes, after a game, we'd start mouthing off to the boys on the other team. Our sneakers were a source of pride, and messing up someone's sneakers was grounds for trouble.

Bobby would always break it up, and talk to us about why showing respect is the right path. He'd explain how we treat others affects our life. Bobby not only coached us in sports, but in how to become men.

"By acting with respect, you're showing people who you are," he'd say. "Once you react to a situation, you've made a decision for how to use your energy. A negative plus a negative equals a negative. A positive is the only way to change the equation."

Bobby was a good mentor because he had been through a lot in his life. He was from Perth Amboy, the youngest of ten kids and his father passed away when he was young. Bobby achieved success in basketball, and then threw it all away. Yet, he had gained wisdom through his mistakes, and he was committed to sharing how he'd been somewhere we never wanted to be. He taught us how to grow up stronger and better.

"Be kind to someone every day," was another bit of wisdom he'd share, "Be slow to speak and quick to listen." He taught us that eye-to-eye contact was of singular importance, affecting your whole life's journey. We were used to looking off, or looking at the ground when addressing people. He would interrupt, saying, "Look at me when you talk to me, young man."

Once, I got in trouble and detention made me miss a game. I was angry and thought I should be able to play anyway. "This is stupid! Why can't I serve the detention tomorrow when there's no game?" I complained.

"Listen, you made the decision that led to this consequence," Bobby said, "A man accepts responsibility for his actions. It was you who put yourself in this situation."

At that time, I was too hard-headed to listen to Bobby. I thought I could do fine using my own judgment, but my judgment was telling me I had all the answers and the rules didn't apply to me. I didn't care about church, or about the other people in the community other than my friends. I rejected his authority as an attempt to control me, not realizing that he was taking the time to mentor me because he saw potential in me. Bobby would take the time to sit with me and work out a plan for how I could do positive things with my time. Then, I'd throw the plan away and go do the opposite.

When people won't listen, eventually they end up in situations where they don't have any choice in the matter. At the end of the day, the people who I had disrespected were the exact people I needed to turn to when I got in trouble. Now I understood that Bobby was trying to help me build character and foster an attitude of respect and appreciation for the people in my life and for myself.

Chapter 7

My last days in Bordentown were nerve-wracking. Whenever someone is about to get released, the other inmates often start finding ways to make life more difficult for that person. Getting in a fight would cost me my freedom. I was always on edge. I tried to stay quiet and keep to myself to avoid any problems, but problems can follow you in a place like that.

The guy who everyone went to to get their hair cut was a friend of mine from Perth Amboy. He would always clean up my hair before my family came for a visitation. One day, he started refusing to cut hair for the black inmates, claiming they 'never paid' and he was tired of it. One day, I happened to be in the day room at the same time as him when about 5 or 6 black guys entered, upset.

"Hey, you have a problem," the leader of the group, Tariq, said. The others chimed in with curses and name-calling. They were slowly closing in around the barber.

I froze. The barber was one of my friends, I couldn't let him get jumped by a big group of men, but I couldn't afford to get into a fight either. I took a deep breath and stepped in the middle of the small room.

"What's the problem?" I asked, even though I knew. "Let's work this out."

"Ain't no working it out! This dude is refusing to serve us! It's not fair and it's racist," Tariq replied.

I looked at the barber. "You know you can't ban all the black inmates from your shop. And you still cut my hair, because you know me."

"Look, I'm sorry but it's not fair to me, either," he responded, "I do the work, spend time cutting their hair and I don't get paid for it!"

"Hector, do any of these guys here owe you money?" I asked.

The barber looked at them for a minute, then pointed at one of the men. "He does, he never paid me for two haircuts already."

I looked back at Tariq. "Hey man, that's not cool either. Not paying him is like stealing from him." Then I turned back to Hector, "but the other four here don't owe you anything, right?"

The barber nodded.

"Okay, Hector, you need to cut hair for these guys here because they didn't do anything wrong. You can ban the one who didn't pay you, but it's not cool to punish all of them for one person's wrongs."

Hector nodded again. "Okay," he said.

I turned back to Tariq. "Is that fair? Your dude over here didn't pay, but you and the rest of your crew can still get haircuts."

Tariq's face was still twisted in anger, but I could see something soften. He paused for a few seconds, but it felt like an eternity. Finally, he nodded. "Let's go," he said to his crew. The men filed out of the day room and I almost collapsed on the floor with relief.

Even though avoiding trouble was stressful, I was also excited that I was about to get out. I was ready to prove that I'm a better person than what I had been labeled. I wrote down goals for myself in my notebook. Now I was faced with the question: Am I really going to do this? If not, then I had just spent my sentence passing time and entertaining myself. I had to be ready to challenge myself, to make sure I really did all of the things I had written and promised myself.

I kept writing in the small, blue notebook. I had to start picturing how I would actually do these things. So I started breaking down my goals into smaller goals that I knew I could reach. My resolution to get a job became concrete steps, like "sign up with a recruiting agency", and "apply for five jobs a day". This was good practice for me and everything I wrote down prepared me to take action.

My time away from Armani made me realize that I hadn't taken full advantage of being a father yet. I had felt too comfortable and I had taken him for granted. I would have never made the choices I did if I had appreciated that responsibility. I never wanted to leave my son's side again, so I had to make choices that reflected that. I also wanted to be good father, so I wrote down things I would do, like "take Armani to the park on your day off".

I looked forward to visits from Jennifer and my sister, although since the time she got turned away, I would get nervous waiting to be called at the door of the visitation room. I wanted to see them, talk to them, because it helped me focus on what I'd do when I got out. I kept sharing with them my goals and telling them I would do better. I saw now how my words were the actions I should have been taking all along. Although I felt a certainty because I was determined and prepared, I knew that I had to prove my words with my actions. I also talked to my friends on the inside about my goals. Many of them had years left to serve. They lent me books to read, like *The 48 Laws of Power*, and told me I had to do good, because I was a good dude.

"No matter what, make sure you never come back here," I heard many times.

Chapter 8

When the day finally came, it was both an incredible joy and a huge wake-up call. The correctional officers came for me in the morning and I boarded a transport van to the court house. I stared out the window, anticipating everything that was to come that day. Outside it was sunny and pleasant. Inside I felt a storm of nerves.

When I got to the court room, I could see my family waiting for me. I wanted to run to them immediately, but I had to wait for the court to process and release me. Under the glaring, fluorescent lights, the judge reviewed my paperwork and released me under "intensive supervision" for the next 18 months.

When the judge clanged his gavel, the first thing I did was run to hug my son. He was 2 now, and he'd grown so much since I saw him last. So many times I'd promised myself I'd never leave him again, but at this moment I felt the truth of that promise. Next was my mother, in a floral dress and a little teary eyed, and then my father. Jennifer had come too, and brought her mom and her cousin.

After speaking to the intensive supervision officer, we left the courthouse and headed straight for my mother's apartment to relax and catch up. As I sat on the old couch in her living room, Mamí told me about the neighborhood goings-on; who had gotten engaged, who had moved, all the drama in the town. Of course, she had had to answer a lot of questions about me, what I did, why I was locked up, what happened. But she didn't harp on it and she didn't want to hear a word about my time in prison.

"That's behind us now, *m'ijo*," she said, "let's talk about the future."

I told her about my notebook, and how much I had planned for this, for my future. Her words were reassuring but her brow knitted as she looked at me, showing a deep concern. Papí reacted differently. He asked me a lot of questions about my time; who I met, whether I held any grudges, what I learned. He was worried about how prison might have changed me. I also told him about my notebook and my plans. He nodded in approval, appearing satisfied. "I'm glad to hear that."

The sun was sinking, casting a soft, warm light as I watched Jennifer and my son descend the stairs from my mom's apartment, leaving me there as they headed home. Then I was left alone with my thoughts.

Doubt has a way of creeping into things. I questioned whether I could do the things I said I would, whether I could live up to the notebook I kept. I thought about my family and how much pain I had caused them. I wanted to be a better role model for my son, to show him a positive life. I wanted to be around, to teach him things, take him to the park, be his father. It was overwhelming. It's hard to return. The pressure of not knowing what will happen, the stress of needing a job, needing a chance, creates a palpable weight on the mind. I felt resolute to pursue my goals, but I knew that now I was up against new problems.

I had been released into an Intensive Supervision Program (ISP), which meant I would be monitored closely for 18 months. I had to get a job within a month and my curfew was 6:00pm. I had to keep a budget, track and report my spending. I had to meet with my supervising officer once a week and take a drug test. I completed community service work every Saturday. Any little mistake would land me back in jail for the full length of the rest of my sentence-- five years. People tried to tell me the program was just a set-up, that they were trying to get people to fail. However, my freedom was in my own hands. I was able to see my son, eat meals with my family, and that motivated me to stay disciplined, to not mess up. I had a lot of responsibility on my shoulders, and I took the challenge seriously.

The officer in charge, Davey, was very straightforward and honest to the point of bluntness. He didn't sugarcoat anything. I liked that, because he let me know exactly what I needed to do in order to succeed. He was very friendly, like a big brother, and some others in the program made the mistake of taking his kindness for weakness. They were sent back to serve their sentences in lock up. Davey treated everyone equally and did not play favorites.

I spent the coming days searching for work. I had to swallow my pride, because a few times I wanted to give up. When I got depressed about it, I'd ask myself, "Am I really going to give up my second chance?" Jennifer had helped me prepare my resume while I was locked up, and one of my friends told me she would look out for jobs for me. I searched the internet and applied at temporary agencies. Within a couple weeks I was back on a loading dock in a warehouse.

How do I explain what it feels like to lose out on a dream? It's not like I thought working in a warehouse was so bad. I had done it, my whole family had done it, but it wasn't the future I had worked so hard for. One of the things that had motivated me to go to college was the chance to help others with opportunities to go further. Now my aspirations were to become a warehouse manager. This was atonement for my mistakes.

The warehouse paid me, then promoted me to shift supervisor, and I was happy to be supporting my family again. My life was simple. I paid the bills, ate dinner with my family and went to church on Sundays. I was grateful to have my life back. At the same time, people in the neighborhood started sending over younger dudes who were struggling, to come talk to me. They would turn up on the loading dock looking for advice, and I would tell them about my story and try to help them steer clear of the path I had taken. I kept it straight with them about exactly what I'd been through, hoping that my struggle would motivate them to do things differently. Then, one day I got a call from Tashi, my high school guidance counselor who had encouraged me in my youth. She was now the Director of a Boys & Girls Club. She had gotten a copy of my resume, and wanted to tell me about an organization called the Jewish Renaissance Foundation. They had an opening for a Programs Coordinator, running a mentoring program for at-risk youth. She thought of me immediately and wanted me to send over my resume.

I was nervous. I didn't want to get my hopes up because I was afraid my record would bar me from the job but I had to take a shot at it. So I started working on my resume and getting feedback from some folks in the neighborhood. When I was satisfied with it, I sent my resume over to Tashi and she submitted it with her recommendation. A week later I had an interview. I was a ball of nerves going in, but once they started talking to me about the job, I knew I was the right fit. My time at the Workforce Development program had exposed me to working with kids, and when they asked me that dreaded question about my record, I didn't hesitate.

"To be quite honest, I think it's something I can use in this job," I told the interviewer, "My story is something these kids will relate to, and I'm prepared to be honest with them about my choices."

I got the job, and I took Jennifer and my son out to dinner to celebrate.

Chapter 9

No matter how much I changed and how much of an impact my prison experience made on my life, I was keenly aware that it could all be taken away again if I made a single mistake. I couldn't get tired of coming home early, slip up and miss my curfew. I had to stay away from the people I had gotten into trouble with because they would only give me opportunities to mess up again. Yes, I needed money, but I had decided to get it the hard way through work, rather than risk going back to prison.

Walking out of the barbershop one day, I saw some guys I knew, Dre and Troy. These were guys that I used to hang out with when I was selling drugs. They were both dealers who'd been locked up a number of times.

"Hey Edison, how you been G? I haven't seen you around in a while," said Troy.

"I'm good, I've just been working, man," I replied.

"He just got out a few months ago," Dre said to Troy, talking about me. "You're still under supervision, huh?" I nodded and said I was.

"When are you trying to get back in?" Dre asked me, looking me in the eye. I half smiled, looking away. He was asking me when I would start dealing again.

"I'm not about that anymore, bro. I'm not going back." I said.

Troy snorted and cracked a grin. "Sure. Okay. I know you're on probation now, E. Once you're out from under that?"

"No, I'm not just talking about while I'm on probation. I'm done man. I'm out."

Dre and Troy looked at each other. "Yeah I heard that before," Troy was still grinning, "Then the money gets tight. Give it time, Edison, you'll be back to the streets."

Now I was starting to laugh, but out of a weird sense of anger. "You not hearing me, brother. I don't care about the money. My life is about my son and my family now. I'm done."

Dre was starting to look angry. "We all got kids. What the hell are you saying, pendejo? You think you're better than us now?"

I was silent. I didn't know what to say. It was my decision, it wasn't about them or anyone else.

Troy snorted again. "Whatever the hell you said, man. People don't change. Hit me up when you're back in the game. Come on, Dre, let's go."

As the two walked off, I stood there stunned. Their attitude was so negative, expecting me to lapse back into their world as if I didn't have free will. What confused and hurt me most was that they thought my choice to change my life for the better somehow involved them. I didn't think I was better or worse than anyone. I was just doing what I had to do for my life.

I didn't see them again, but I ran into others who reacted similarly. There are many people who didn't think change is possible, not just for me, but for themselves or anyone. And sadly, there are also people who will only put down someone who is trying to change their life--as if the effort is an insult to them personally. I was supposed to be a bad kid, a fortune cast before my birth into this world. I couldn't let those negative attitudes get to me. There were several people I called 'friend' back when I had plenty of money, and when I got locked up they weren't there for me. When I asked them to help take care of my family while I was away, they said "Sure," but never called to check up. When I got out and I was broke, they didn't help me. When I decided to earn my money the honest way, they didn't care about me anymore. That's when I realized who my true friends were all along, versus the people who were just with me when times were good.

Jennifer, the mother of my son, was one of those true friends I had known since I was 17, although we decided to take some time apart as a couple. When I got caught, her whole world was turned upside down. She was so hurt by my actions and by my secrecy. "How could you do this while you were living with me and our son? I feel like I don't know who you are anymore," she had said back then. Even though our romantic relationship did not last, Jennifer never left my side as a friend. She stuck by me through the most difficult time of both our lives, driving an hour and a half each way to see me in prison, putting money in my commissary, helping me with my resume. She did all this while she was figuring out how to take care of Armani by herself, supporting them on her small income and living as a single mother for the first time. The depth of her sacrifice and her strength humbled me. I had to make it up to her.

My parents, too, had never abandoned their son, even though my mother refused to come see me in prison. She didn't want to remember her son that way, and even though I missed her, on some level I understood. Both my parents had endured the questions and judgments of friends and neighbors, some who said I'd always been a bad apple, a troublemaker. They had fought back, defending me even as they were dealing with their own disappointment in my behavior.

I apologized to my son, too, although he was too young to really understand. He was the single biggest driver of my motivation to grow up and be responsible. I swore to him I would never leave his side again. Even though Jennifer and I weren't together anymore, we had agreed to always put Armani first, and we learned how to co-parent and show that you don't have to be together to get along. More than anything, we wanted to show Armani that he was loved by both his parents, and to teach him that family is the most important thing of all.

It was hard for me to get over the fact I had brought so much pain upon my family. I saw very clearly now that I had taken them for granted, caring more about what others thought of me, trying to impress these so-called 'friends'. I had put my family through hell, and they had stayed by my side while those other people left me. How could I ever repay them? I didn't know how, but I swore I'd never turn my back on my family again. That motivated me to work harder, to be better, not for me but for them. The pain pushed me to be successful so I could make them proud again.

When I saw my mentor Bobby again, he didn't have much time for my apologies. "You made a mistake. It happens," he said, "The important question is: What are you going to do now?"

At first, the answer to that question was simple. I had written down everything I was going to do. But once I had a achieved some of my goals, like getting a job and spending time with my son, I started to get lazier about writing in my notebook. My probabtion officer, Davey, noticed and he started having me record what I did every day that was productive and a step towards my goals. He pushed me to keep setting goals, and this helped me stay focused on what I needed to do. He kept reminding me that it was all in my hands, "If you put your mind to something and you really believe in it, there's no way you shouldn't be able to achieve it. Before anyone can believe in you, you have to believe in yourself."

One of the things I had to do was humble myself. I couldn't desire fancy things, and I had to get used to the difference between needing something and wanting something. I have to focus on today: doing well at my job, networking, getting things right. One of the hardest things for me was asking for help. That was how I got myself into trouble in the first place--I didn't want to ask anyone to help me, I wanted to take care of myself. Now I realized we are meant to lean on each other, and there's nothing wrong with asking the people who want to help you for some help when you need it. No one is meant to live life alone.

Over time, Davey gave me more and more freedom, like leeway to stay out past 6:00 pm. Each time, he'd remind me about my little boy, to keep me on my toes and thinking about not making mistakes. His role was to decide when to allow a little more rope, and it was your job to decide whether or not to hang yourself with it. I saw many people get sent back to prison because they couldn't wait to get back in the club, or to smoke weed, or because they got comfortable and thought they could pull one over on Davey and not get caught. They always got caught, and they ended up serving longer sentences for failing to follow the program's strict rules. In many ways, it was tougher than jail. Sure, you get the freedom to see your family, to go to work and earn money, but you have to have a lot of self-control, and you have to be able to earn the officer's trust. That's why Davey would always remind me of my son, my reason to stay out of prison, because to get through it, you have to want your freedom more than anything else.

I was open with my co-workers about the ISP program, and they became big supporters of mine. Yudelkis, Malle, and Sherri would encourage me whenever they saw me writing in my journal during lunch, or working on my budget. When we had events that ran later than 6:00pm, they'd call Davey and ask him for special permission on my behalf. They were all working in programs focused on helping at-risk youth become successful in life, so they really understood and wanted to see me succeed. I kept hearing, "Edison, you should tell kids about your experiences, so they don't make the same mistakes as you."

When I reached the end of the ISP program, I was the first person in eighteen years to complete it perfectly. I received an award at the graduation ceremony, and as I stood in front of the judges there, I thought back to the time I stood in front of that judge who was so disappointed in me. I was overwhelmed with emotion, feeling proud that I not only turned it around and completed the program, but that I took it to the next level. I felt a surge of appreciation, too, for all the people who were there for me, my support system, my family, my mentors, my coworkers. This day was their day, too.

Once I had total freedom, I realized I had lost the taste for things like partying or going to the clubs. It was very eye-opening to go back with a new perspective, and I realized it wasn't for me anymore. Where once I would be excited to go 'hang with my boys', now I felt like we were just sitting around doing nothing.

I really started sticking to myself, taking the time to learn about myself and work on creating the future I envisioned in my head. I realized that, with this new focus, things that would have once been a big sacrifice were now simply things I wanted to do. For instance, saving money. I used to buy what I wanted, or if I didn't have the money I would complain. Now I see the difference between what I want and what I need, and how saving money helps me achieve my dreams. Once I had gotten lazy about writing my goals down in my notebook, and I had to be required to by another person. Now, making goals and accomplishing them made me feel like someone, like I can do anything if I keep striving and never give up.

Spending time giving back to the community is another thing that might have once seemed like a big sacrifice of my time, but now I see how fulfilling it is. I learned that giving back is what gives you more life. A selfish person cannot be a happy person, and I was finding more and more that I was happy.

Chapter 10

I stayed in touch with Tashi after she helped me find the job at the Jewish Renaissance Foundation. We talked a lot about mentoring and the current programs out there for youth. Tashi truly values giving back, and through her I was motivated to make that a priority in my life. I was still friends with Sandy, who led the trips I used to go on when I was young, and we talked frequently about working with at-risk youth.

I also thought a lot about the role Bobby Nicholson played in my life. Bobby was helping out coaching basketball at a basketball league program run by the JRF. Bobby was a great mentor who demonstrated what being a grown man and a father meant. I didn't listen to his advice as a young man, but his advice stayed with me, like a seed planted to grow later. His role was influential, even if it wasn't immediate. Another person of great influence to me was Pastor Paul. When I first moved to the Projects, he was always there to talk to and provide advice.

My experiences working with at-risk youth in the Civic Justice Corps, paired with the support of my mentors, motivated me and inspired me to create a new mentoring program for lost youth. I started thinking about all the kids I could reach, who were struggling to find the path to success. I saw a huge need in my community for a mentoring program led by positive role models. That dream and vision motivated me to start *B-Men*, a youth program targeting those kids who were at risk and had been turned away from other programs. *B-Men* strives to help these at risk youth "be men" hence the name. I was fortunate to meet someone with the same vision, Linda. Linda knew the process and helped me become an official organization. I was excited when we received the state paperwork, and I felt how real it was.

I decided I would not turn kids away, because I had been turned away from so many programs--for fighting, for getting in trouble, for not doing my school work. Those were signs I was in trouble, yet it meant I couldn't participate in the programs that could possibly help me. Second chances weren't available so I was left to the street. Being routinely shut out leads to predictable outcomes. With *B-Men* I decided to take a different approach: If no one is helping you, I will help you. We focus on life skills, resume building, and college. I make sure education is number one. I decided to make *B-Men* about second chances, an ideal I found so important.

I wanted the program to create bonds, like a family, so I made it a 10-week program. After 10 weeks, the young men would receive certificates and be recognized for their accomplishment, but they would be welcomed back for another 10 weeks if they chose. Growth is a process of iteration, so coming back actually means you are benefiting. Even if you hear the same speaker, you will listen to him or her with new ears and a new perspective. At *B-Men*, when we start pushing you to leave the program, it's out of love because it's time for you to start spreading your wings and achieve.

The program started in October 2013, with six kids and myself. Today, I am one of five mentors in Perth Amboy alone; there are three mentors in Jersey City and also one in Plainfield. Each mentor leads a 10-week program with a group of youth. We've reached 40 young men since we started. My biggest challenge in learning to be a mentor was having patience. I wanted to see the kids in my program change overnight, even though I knew that was not how fast I changed. When I started talking to my first group about their goals, I realized I was talking to kids whose goals were simply to survive, to not get arrested. No one ever told them they could excel at anything. I knew that each of them could do anything he set his mind to, but I realized I had to calculate the investment: four months to get his GED, at least two years or more to get a college degree. Through all that, these young men needed help finding answers to questions such as, "Is it okay that I grew up without a father?" and "Can you tell me I can make it, coming from my hood?"

Not only could I not expect change overnight, but I realized that we had to go at their pace, not my pace. I thought back to my youth, and how teachers always pressured me to work at their pace, asking me to turn in work rather than asking how I felt about finishing the work. When you don't do the work properly, they tell you that you're not going to go anywhere in life. Then you act out because that's a terrible thing to believe. So I had to let each young man work at his pace, help him explore the challenges he faced with patience, and place value on the process, without losing sight of the outcome.

While learning how to be a mentor was one challenge, I also had to learn how to lead this new program and get the community involved. My former mentors and many friends supported me, and many wanted to join in and help. I was also met with a good deal of disinterest from leaders who suspected I was somehow doing this all for myself, even though I wasn't asking them for anything but to show their face to some young people in the community. Over time, I let the youth become the messenger, because they can speak for themselves better than anyone.

The parents of the youth in *B-Men* also spread the word. When a mother or father comes to tell me "Thank you for dealing with my son, after nobody else would," I say, "Tell other parents how *B-Men* helped." Perth Amboy is a small town, and these are parents who before were saying they couldn't get control of their son, how they wanted to send him off to boot camp, how they were at the end of their rope and couldn't take it anymore. Now they're saying someone helped their son get on the right path? People pay attention to that.

One of my first mentees just recently earned his Associate Degree. When John started with *B-Men*, he was one of the toughest kids I dealt with. He had a bad attitude and a lack of motivation. He was disrespectful, and he acted like he didn't care about anything, at all. After he was in the program, I sat him down and had serious conversation with him about where he was heading. I explained to him that jail was not the right place for him. When John started putting his energy into positive things, his tough guy attitude turned into determination. He has earned his GED, became a father, and worked his way through college, earning his degree.

Carlos, another early *B-Men* mentee, had a dream when I asked him about careers: he wanted to start his own marketing firm and begin creating websites. He just didn't know where to start. At the time, *B-Men* did not have a website, so we challenged him to the project. His first attempt was great, so we sat him down and talked more seriously about it. Today, he manages our website full-time, helping us promote news and events, and he uses the *B-Men* site as an addition to his work portfolio. Beyond reaching leaders or parents, the successes of young men like John and Carlos show other youth that this program is for them.

Chapter 11

Visions are unmixing things, things that are unknown, you stand alone in the presence of any man known. You disperse in your direction that makes you feel free even if it's standing away from everyone, including me. That's something. Something to see, something to realize and one day believe that the other things you see take hold onto the life you soon wish to exceed in a sense that the wondrous thoughts of physical action make you stronger than the feet you stand on. Here's now, there's you, there's all that you did that left marks, marks of guidance, marks of life, marks of laughter and vivacious memories that people love. Drove into the center of success and woke up into a world that lets you witness everything from first sight. God above. ~ Yanel Rivera

One of my supporters was my childhood friend Richard Pryce. Growing up, Richie was like a brother to me. His family lived in the same building as I did, and we hung out with the same kids after school. He loved to come over to eat at my apartment, and would often ask me, "What's your mom cooking today?" Richie would clown and make jokes, but he was also very smart and quick to anger. He would talk like he was Michael Jordan when we played basketball, showing off, but he was a good player. He dressed fashionably and he loved to debate who was the best rapper. We got in trouble and got in fights together, and we got kicked out of programs together.

Richie also went to college, and when I started *B-Men*, Richie was also finding ways to give back to our community. He helped mentor kids specifically on how to get into college. He'd help them get prepared and understand how to get financial aid, and gave them practical advice about school that their parents couldn't tell them.

When I started up *B-Men*, Richie was supportive from the beginning. The energy that we had for helping others was special. We talked often about mentoring, and how complementary our programs were. *B-Men* focuses on taking on leadership and responsibility, regardless of whether or not college is in the plan. I just want to keep kids off the streets. For those young men in the program who are planning for college, Richie was a great resource. We discussed putting our programs together, so that Richie could run the college mentoring arm of *B-Men*, but he told me he wasn't ready just yet. He felt that he needed some time to get some things together before we joined forces. He was really proud of me when I told him I was working on my book. He wanted to read it and he told me he really wanted to get to that point and write a book as well. I wanted him to know that there was no competition, and that I encouraged him and wanted him to get his book started.. I felt we could both win when we do good things together. I was excited for him, his plans, and the possibility of us collaborating. I was patient with my friend, letting him be ready in his own time.

One cool February evening, Richie was out for the night in a club when a man confronted him and the two men left the club. They only made it to the sidewalk outside the club before the man pulled out a gun. He shot Richie, and my dear friend lost his life at the hospital.

I still wake up every day and ask, "Why Richie?" He did so much to help people. His loss was felt not just by his family and his friends, but it truly left a hole in the community. We'll never know how many lives he could have changed if he was still here, but it would have been many. He died for something that could have been solved without violence. Situations like this happen every day. Young men are so quick to pick up a gun and pull the trigger. The man that killed Richie threw his own life away at the same time. He will spend his life in prison.

After this tragedy, my two close friends, Terrance & Brett, became closer and realized that we needed to be there for each other as true friends and to not let anything break our friendship. There are no winners in situations like this, only profound loss. If you ever think that violence may be the only way to solve a situation you find yourself in, please find someone to talk to.

Chapter 12

Every choice has a consequence. You don't have to make a mistake before you know it's a mistake. You don't have to be a follower. You don't have to sell drugs. More importantly, you don't have to give up on dreaming, but you do have to put in the work to make those dreams a reality. "The dream is free, but the hustle is sold separately."

My story, my pain, can help you. You don't have to make the same mistakes I made. I thought I was slick, selling on the side, hanging out with the baddest dudes, parties, girls - but that life didn't work out for me. It gave me a felony and nearly wrecked my life. I learned that I should have been paying attention to the people who would stay by my side through thick and thin, putting effort into being a good father, investing time in getting a better job. When I mentor, I present these two alternate paths I've traveled and I ask: How are the streets going to save you? No one has an answer for that. For a long time I felt like people were waiting for me to make another mistake, assuming I was still a bad apple. I still run into people who are genuinely surprised at the impact I'm making. They wonder how I was able to do that, how I made that positive change.

I give thanks to God for the role that my faith has played in setting me upon this path. My life began to change truly when I allowed God into it. If I believe and I strive, God never lets me down. I am humbled by God's role in my life and grateful for every person who prayed for me non-stop, especially Nati's mother (Jennifer's aunt).

Some people think I'm crazy. They ask me why I'm hanging around Perth Amboy helping kids when I could be working for a Fortune 500 company and traveling the world. I tell them what I do, I do for my son. He doesn't need a father who's gone all the time, working to afford a big, empty house. Instead, my son will have a father who shows him how to be a kind, grateful, and generous person. He has a father who loves and takes care of people. That is worth more than money could ever buy.

When I was a boy, my parents had to rely on charity to make Christmas happen every year. They were grateful for the program that brought wrapped toys to youth in the projects, but I felt confused and ungrateful because it just didn't have any meaning to me. A man would show up dressed as Santa Claus, with a black garbage bag full of the same toys as last year, and he'd pass them out dutifully without talking about the meaning of Christmas, then send us home without any celebration. One particular year, I was listening to this Santa Claus talk about why he does this every year. I got frustrated and blurted out, "Then why do you give us the same toys every year?"

The kids around me looked shocked and amused. Santa Claus was flabbergasted.

"What… do you… You know you are very ungrateful, young man."

I continued to protest. "I'm not being ungrateful, I just want to know the truth!"

The other kids were now laughing, unable to believe I had the nerve to stand up to him. Their amusement was making Santa angry. "Look, there's a lot you don't understand yet. You're lucky to get these gifts! This is the best we can do. You ought to be grateful!"

"When I grow up," I said, "I'm going to give back to my community, and it won't just be the same toy over and over again!"

Santa snorted. "Good luck with that, kid."

I am proud to say that every year I put together a team of volunteers to make Thanksgiving and Christmas special for some of the needy families in our neighborhood. I ask for donations from people, from bodegas, from shops. On Thanksgiving, there's food to eat and a DJ to help celebrate. For Christmas, I invite NFL players to come speak and take photos, and the kids get different toys every year. The families that participate are so grateful, but what's difficult is that I can only serve 300. I send a letter to the area schools and ask them to identify the two students in their school with the greatest need, but every year I meet families who don't make it, who say, "I pray that my family gets picked next year." It makes me feel bad, but there's only so much I can do. Yvonne Moore, my assistant, is key to making everything running smoothly. I encourage everyone to take responsibility and be a Christmas blessing to someone in need.

I came from the bottom, from struggle, from no sense of the positive. I have to remain humble and help others going through the same situation. When a young person says to me, "You've changed my life," it makes me feel like a rich man. It means I've helped stop them from hurting themselves. It means that person will live a happier life and they won't cause their families the pain and suffering that my family and so many others go through.

Although I've shared my story with you, this book is not really about me. It's about you. When will you change? I challenge you to ask yourself:

- What am I doing that I know is wrong? What can I do better?
- Am I working as hard as I could be on making a dream become reality?
- Are there people in my life that I am taking for granted? How could I let them know I care about them and appreciate them?
- How am I giving back to the community? Am I taking more than I give?

The truth is that your decisions affect your life, and the decision to find a mentor (or become a mentor) is the first step in making real change.

Thank you for reading this book. I challenge you to do more to be your best.

ABOUT THE AUTHOR

Edison A. Jaquez is the Program Coordinator for the Civic Justice Corps at the Jewish Renaissance Foundation, where he is responsible for program planning, and training while working with at-risk male youth between the ages of 16 and 24. In addition to his current position, Edison is the CEO of B-Men and Co-Founder of BYOUtiful, mentoring organizations designed to enhance the lives of today's youth. He is also a motivational speaker traveling throughout the state sharing his story with audiences young and old. Edison lives in Perth Amboy, New Jersey and is the proud father of his son, Armani.

For more information, please visit www.bmenmentoring.org.

Made in the USA
Middletown, DE
26 September 2015